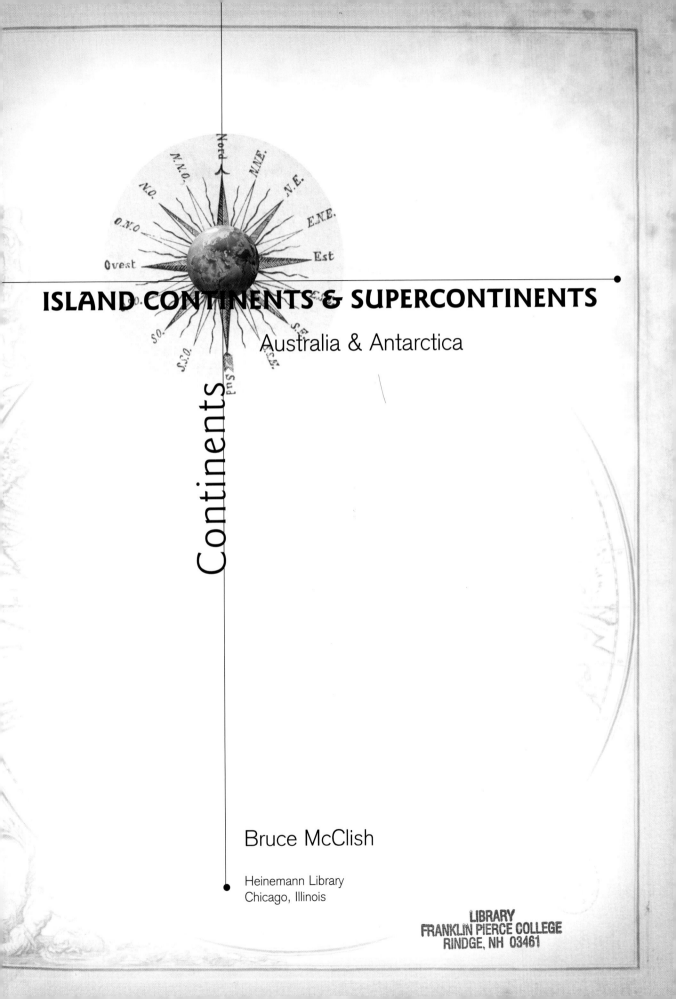

ISLAND CONTINENTS & SUPERCONTINENTS

Australia & Antarctica

Continents

Bruce McClish

Heinemann Library
Chicago, Illinois

Designed by Stella Vassiliou
Maps and diagrams by Pat Kermode and Stella Vassiliou
Printed in China by Wing King Tong Co. Ltd.

07 06 05 04 03
10 9 8 7 6 5 4 3 2 1

Library of Congress Cataloging-in-Publication Data
McClish, Bruce.
  Island continents and supercontinents : Australia and Antarctica /
Bruce McClish.
     v. cm. -- (Continents)
Summary: Island continents -- Introducing Australia -- Australia: land and landforms -- Australia: climate, plants and animals -- Australia: history and culture -- Introducing Antarctica -- Antarctica: land and landforms -- Antarctica: climate, plants and animals -- Antarctica: discovery and exploration -- The making of island continents -- Changes in climate -- Isolation and wildlife.
Includes bibliographical references (p.   ).
  ISBN 1-4034-2989-8 (lib. bdg. : hardcover) 1-4034-4245-2 (paperback)
  1. Continents--Juvenile literature. 2. Islands--Juvenile literature.
3. Australia--Juvenile literature. 4. Antarctica--Juvenile literature.
[1. Australia. 2. Antarctica. 3. Continents. 4. Islands.] I. Title. II.
Continents (Chicago, Ill.)
  G920 .M33 2003
  994--dc21
                          2002011597

Acknowledgments
The author and publishers are grateful to the following for permission to reproduce copyright material:
pp. 5, 11 (left), 18 (bottom) PhotoDisc; pp. 7 (all), 9, 27 Tourism New South Wales; p. 8 Tourism Victoria; p. 12 Not Bad Design & Print, www.notbad.com.au; p. 15 Australian Picture Library; p. 16 Rod Ledingham; pp. 17, 19, 22 Auscape/Jean-Paul Ferrero; p. 18 (top) ANT Photo Library/Jonathan Chester; p. 21 by permission of the National Library of Australia; p. 25 (left) Coo-ee Picture Library; p. 25 (right) © Natural History Museum (London); p. 26 Auscape/Dennis Harding; p. 28 Nature Focus/Carl Bento; p. 29 Greening Australia.

Cover photograph of outback New South Wales, Australia, supplied by Tourism New South Wales.

The author would like to thank: Avi Olshina, geologist; Peter Nunan, geography teacher; Craig Campbell, researcher; and Jenny McClish, researcher and contributing author.

Every effort has been made to contact copyright holders of any material reproduced in this book. Any omissions will be rectified in subsequent printings if notice is given to the publisher.

Some words are shown in bold, **like this.** You can find out what they mean by looking in the glossary.

Contents

Island
CONTINENTS

A continent is a huge **landmass** on Earth's surface. Earth has seven major continents: Europe, Asia, Africa, North America, South America, Australia, and Antarctica.

Most continents lie near—or are even connected to—some other continent. For example, Europe lies near Africa, and North America is connected to South America. Only two continents are completely separate from all the others and surrounded by water. They are Australia and Antarctica.

In some ways, Australia and Antarctica seem very different from each other. One continent is known for its hot deserts and sunny beaches, while the other is known for its massive **glaciers** and frozen seas. But aside from **climate,** Australia and Antarctica have a lot in common. Both are among the smallest three continents. Besides being the only island continents, they are the only continents that lie completely in the **Southern Hemisphere.** Their seasons are reversed from those of the **Northern Hemisphere.** Australia and Antarctica were also the last continents to be explored and settled by Europeans.

The Gondwana connection

Australia and Antarctica are island continents today. However, millions of years ago, they were connected to each other. At one time, they were part of a massive supercontinent called Gondwana. This supercontinent was made up of other huge landmasses, including Africa, South America, and India—which is part of Asia today. In ancient times, plants and animals from Australia could easily move into Antarctica—as well as many other parts of Gondwana.

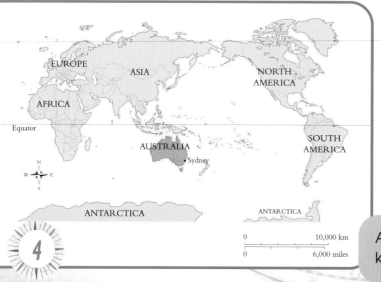

Australia and Antarctica are known as the island continents.

4

About 200 million years ago, Gondwana began to break apart. Forces from deep within Earth caused different parts of the supercontinent to move slowly apart. Because of this movement, Australia and Antarctica separated and each became **isolated.** While continents such as Africa and South America eventually moved closer to other continents, Australia and Antarctica moved into remote parts of the ocean. Australia moved north toward the warm **equator.** Antarctica remained close to the South Pole. Even though they are separate today, Australia and Antarctica still share certain kinds of wildlife.

Oceania

There are thousands of islands in the central and southern Pacific Ocean. They together are known as Oceania. This includes islands such as Samoa, Tonga, and Fiji. Some **geographers** say that Australia is part of Oceania, along with islands such as Papua New Guinea and New Zealand. With these included, the total land area of Oceania covers more than 3.3 million sq mi (8.5 million sq km). Some geographers believe Oceania should be considered a continent, with Australia as its largest island. Yet Australia is by far the greatest part of Oceania, covering more than 90 percent of its land surface.

Different kinds of penguins live in Australia and Antarctica, as well as on the coasts and islands of South America and Africa.

Introducing
AUSTRALIA

Australia is the smallest and flattest continent. It is the only continent that is also a country, with its entire **landmass** controlled by one government.

The name *Australia* comes from the Latin word *australis,* which means "southern." The English nicknamed Australia "the land down under," because it is located so far south. The word *Australasia* is sometimes used to include Australia, New Zealand, and certain islands in the Pacific Ocean.

Most of Australia is dry and thinly populated. The country has a shortage of water. Even so, Australia's coastal areas can be green and **fertile,** especially in the southeast. Australia's largest cities are located in these coastal regions.

Australia is a very unique continent.

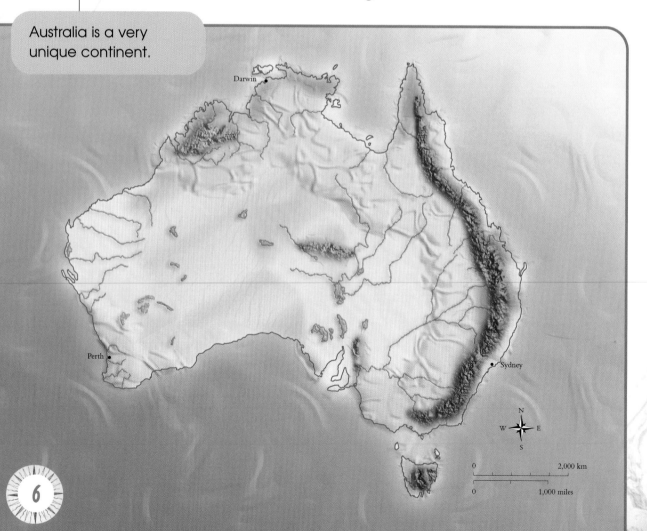

Darwin

Perth

Sydney

N
W · E
S

| 0 | | 2,000 km |
| 0 | | 1,000 miles |

Australia has a surprising variety of scenery, including snowy mountains, lush rain forests, sandy beaches, and the world's longest chain of coral reefs and islands—known as the Great Barrier Reef. Australian animals, such as the platypus, kangaroo, and koala bear, are unlike those found on any other continent.

Australia has productive industries such as farming, mining, and tourism. Most of the people who live there have a high **standard of living.**

Australia has productive farming industries.

Australia: facts and figures

Area:	3 million sq m (7.7 million sq km)
Climate:	temperate and tropical
Population:	19,231,000
Highest peak:	Mt. Kosciusko—7,300 ft (2,228 m) above sea level
Lowest point:	Lake Eyre—52.5 ft (16 m) below sea level. Lake Eyre is also Australia's largest lake (salt), at 3,475 sq mi (9,000 sq km).
Longest river:	Murray–Darling river system—1,450 mi (3,750 km)
Biggest desert:	Great Victoria Desert—150,000 sq mi (388,500 sq km)
Crop products:	wheat, fruits, sugar, barley, oats, rice, vegetables, cotton, **timber**
Animals and animal products:	sheep and wool, beef and dairy cattle, chickens and eggs, fish, and shellfish
Mineral products:	copper, gold, lead, silver, **iron ore,** zinc, nickel, **bauxite,** coal, natural gas, petroleum, and others
Other products and industries:	electrical equipment, clothing and textiles, **pharmaceuticals,** chemicals, steel, automobiles, aircraft, ships, processed food, paper, tourism

Most Australians can enjoy sunny weather and outdoor fun throughout the year.

Land and Landforms

Much of Australia's land surface is very old and worn. There are mountains, but few of them are very high. Australia is the only continent that does not have **glaciers** or an active volcano.

Mountains

Australia's biggest mountains lie along its east coast. The Great Dividing Range—also called the Great Divide—is the continent's longest and highest mountain chain. It stretches along in an arched shape from the northeastern tip of the continent all the way to the south. Mt. Kosciusko, Australia's highest mountain, is part of the Great Dividing Range. Many slopes in this range are covered with forests and woodlands. In the southern part of the range, there are **alpine** meadows and winter snowfields.

West of the Great Dividing Range, and across most of the continent, the land is low and flat. There are some mountains in the west, but they are not very high when compared with larger mountains on other continents. Millions of years ago, these Australian mountains were much higher, but they were gradually worn down by **erosion.**

The Grampion mountain range is in southern Australia.

The Central Lowlands

Plains are found in most coastal areas of Australia, but much wider and lower plains are found in the central lowlands of Australia. The central lowlands lie west of the Great Dividing Range and extend into central Australia. This area is dry, with huge regions of desert, salt lakes, and scrub land made up of small shrubs. There are no large cities in the central lowlands.

Ancient landscapes

Most of central and Western Australia is covered with a very ancient rock surface. Some of these rocks are billions of years old. Much of the land is flat and dry, but it is higher in **elevation** than the central lowlands. In fact, there are many hills and low mountains there. Central and Western Australia are important regions for mining and cattle grazing.

Rivers and water

Rivers are very important in a dry continent such as Australia. Rivers on the eastern side of the Great Dividing Range generally flow a short distance before emptying into the sea. Rivers on the western side can flow for thousands of miles across the dry plains. Most of these rivers do not flow at all during the dry season.

Australia has great natural stores of underground water. These are useful in dry areas without a river, especially for **livestock.** The underground water can be pumped or sometimes flows naturally to the surface.

Diary of a continent

▶ **280 million years ago**
Much of Australia is covered with glaciers in a great southern **ice age.**

▶ **200 million years ago**
Australia is part of the Gondwana supercontinent, along with Antarctica, Africa, and South America.

▶ **150 million years ago**
Gondwana breaks up.

▶ **100 million years ago**
Central Australia is flooded by seas during the **Age of Reptiles.**

▶ **40 million years ago**
Australia tears away from Antarctica and begins to drift north.

▶ **60 000–40 000 years ago**
Humans cross a **land bridge** from Papua New Guinea to inhabit Australia.

▶ **1788**
Europeans start permanent settlement in Australia.

Most land in Australia is flat and dry.

9

Climate, Plants, and Animals

Climate

Australia is known as a warm and sunny land. The northern third of the continent lies in the **tropical** zone, near Earth's **equator,** where temperatures are warm or hot throughout the year.

The southern part of Australia lies in the **temperate** zone, where the weather can be much cooler. During the winter, snow falls on the mountains in southeastern Australia, while rain falls on the coastal areas. Even deserts in the temperate zone can get cold during the winter months. However, southern Australia has plenty of mild and sunny weather—even in winter—and temperatures during the summer months can be as warm as tropical temperatures. Australians are able to grow crops and enjoy outdoor activities year-round. **Droughts,** floods, and fires are common natural disasters in Australia. They can happen any time of the year.

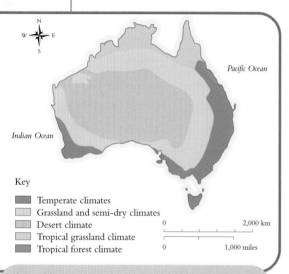

Key

- Temperate climates
- Grassland and semi-dry climates
- Desert climate
- Tropical grassland climate
- Tropical forest climate

Pacific Ocean

Indian Ocean

0   2,000 km

0   1,000 miles

Australia has plenty of sunny weather.

Acacia and eucalyptus trees

Two types of plants, acacia trees and eucalyptus trees are common throughout Australia. Both of these plants have **evergreen** features and sometimes colorful flowers. Eucalyptus trees have leaves and bark that can burn very easily. They often cause fires to spread in warm, dry weather.

Unique animals

Australia is an island continent, and its animals have been **isolated** from the rest of the world for millions of years. Many Australian animals are found nowhere else. Australia has more **marsupials** and **monotremes** than any other continent. Marsupials are pouched mammals, such as kangaroos, koala bears, and possums. Monotremes, such as the platypus and echidna, are the only mammals that lay eggs.

Birds and reptiles

Many Australian birds, such as the large, flightless emu, are not found anywhere else on Earth. There are also many kinds of parrots, including cockatoos and colorful birds such as rosellas, parakeets, and lorikeets.

The warm weather of Australia suits many kinds of reptiles, including snakes, lizards, turtles, and crocodiles. Australia has some of the largest lizards and most venomous snakes in the world.

Introduced animals

Some wild animals do not belong in Australia. These animals were brought to Australia by Europeans. Rabbits, foxes, goats, pigs, horses, cattle, cats, dogs, camels, and cane toads are examples of introduced animals. They are not harmful in their **native** environments, but when they run wild in Australia they cause great harm—preying on native animals or eating or trampling the native plants.

Grasslands and open woodlands
- red kangaroo
- gray kangaroo
- hairy-nosed wombat
- echidna
- brown snake
- goanna
- frilled-neck lizard
- bearded dragon
- emu
- mallee fowl
- wedge-tailed eagle
- galah

Temperate forests
- Tasmanian devil
- native cat
- koala
- ring-tailed possum
- sugar glider
- platypus
- common wombat
- lyrebird
- tawny frogmouth

- kookaburra
- funnel-web spider

Deserts
- dingo
- wallaroo
- bilby
- desert rat-kangaroo
- marsupial mole
- mulga parrot
- sandswimming skink
- mountain devil
- death adder
- waterholding frog
- desert wolf spider

Tropical forests
- tree kangaroo
- flying fox
- spotted cuscus
- cassowary
- bower bird
- Atlas moth

The kangaroo is one of Australia's many unique animals.

History and Culture

People first came to Australia more than 40,000 years ago. They came from islands to the north of the continent. The earliest societies were those of two groups—the Aboriginal people and Torres Strait Islanders. Aboriginal people covered the widest area of Australia and were spread across the entire continent. Different Aboriginal groups lived in desert, mountain, forest, and coastal environments. These groups were **nomadic,** constantly traveling from camp to camp, hunting and gathering food in different places. Torres Strait Islanders, on the other hand, always lived close to the sea. They made their living by fishing, hunting, trading, and farming. These two groups of native peoples still live in Australia today.

Convict settlers

European settlement began in Australia in 1788. Most of the earliest settlers were **convicts** and soldiers from England. They lived mainly on the east coast, and did not travel far. But by the early 1800s, there were major cities in the south and Western Australia. Settlers pushed farther inland, where they established more farms and towns. The land was used for wheat and for raising sheep and cattle. The Aboriginal people were steadily pushed off their land. Fighting sometimes broke out between Aboriginal and settler groups.

Some Aboriginal groups still live in traditional ways and speak traditional languages.

Mineral wealth

Gold was discovered in eastern Australia during the mid-1800s. The gold rush that followed attracted hundreds of thousands of new settlers to the continent, and many new towns and cities sprang up near the gold fields. Even after the gold rush ended, discoveries of uranium, **iron ore,** silver, **bauxite,** nickel, and petroleum made Australia an important mining country in the 1900s.

Australia today

Although Australia lies close to the Asian continent, most of the people who live in Australia have a European background and speak English. Their culture is similar to that of the United States, Great Britain, and New Zealand. The **standard of living** is generally high, with a relaxed lifestyle. There have never been any major wars or **famines** in Australia. Families are generally not as closely tied as they are in Asia. It is not unusual for people to take jobs, go to schools, or settle in homes that are far away from their parents.

Facts about living in
Australia

- Australia has good schools and hospitals, as well as excellent transportation and communication systems.
- Along with farming and mining, tourism has become an important Australian industry.
- Not all Australians belong to an English-speaking, European culture. Aboriginal groups still speak traditional languages in some parts of Australia and there are many immigrants who speak another language, such as Turkish or Vietnamese.
- More than four out of every five Australians live in a city area.
- Most Australians belong to Christian religions, but do not regularly attend church.

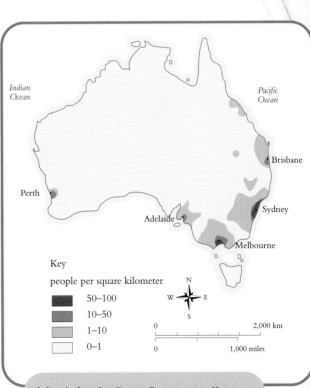

Most Australians live near the south-eastern corner of the continent.

Introducing
ANTARCTICA

Antarctica is the fifth-largest of Earth's seven continents. It is Earth's southernmost continent, lying over the South Pole. Antarctica is a harsh land. Of all the continents, it is the coldest, stormiest, windiest, and iciest.

The name *Antarctica* comes from the Greek word *antartik*, which means "opposite the Arctic." Antarctica does lie opposite the Arctic region, which is around the North Pole. Antarctica is colder than the Arctic. Antarctica is so cold that few plants and animals can survive on the land. This means that most of the continent is a desert—a cold desert—with landforms covered by ice, snow, or bare rock. Antarctica has some amazing scenery, however, including ice cliffs, towering mountains, active volcanoes, and the world's longest **glaciers**.

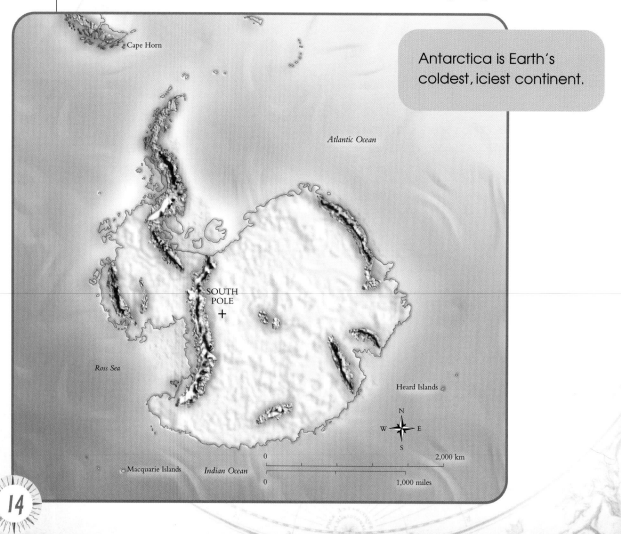

Antarctica is Earth's coldest, iciest continent.

Antarctica was the last continent to be discovered and explored. It is still the only continent with no permanent human residents. However, hundreds of scientists from many different countries are stationed there to study glaciers, rocks, plants, animals, and the weather. Increasing numbers of tourists also visit Antarctica to see its wonders.

Antarctica: facts and figures

Area: 5.4 million sq mi (14 million sq km)

Climate: polar

Population: no permanent residents

Highest peak: Vinson Massif 16,860 ft (5,140 m) above sea level

Lowest point: Bentley Subglacial Trench 8,330 ft (2,538 m) below sea level

Thickest ice: 15,750 ft (4,800 m)

Longest glacier: Lambert Glacier 435 mi (700 km)

Products: fish, krill

Most of the world's ice is found on the continent of Antarctica.

Land and Landforms

Almost all of Antarctica is covered by thick layers of ice. Some of this ice has piled up higher than mountains or spread out into the sea. In fact, there is so much ice that it adds a great deal to the continent's size and height. If it were not for the ice, Antarctica would be the smallest continent.

The Antarctic ice cap

The vast covering of ice over most of Antarctica is called an ice cap or ice sheet. The Antarctic ice cap covers many of the continent's landforms—hills, mountains, valleys, plains, and lake beds. The ice cap can be more than two and one half miles (four kilometers) thick.

Glaciers

Antarctica has many **glaciers.** These masses of ice move downhill, toward the sea. Glaciers move more slowly than water, but they are very powerful. They pick up rocks, scrape them against the ground, carve away mountains, and bulldoze the land. When a glacier meets the sea, it can break up and form **icebergs.** Large icebergs can float for years in the sea before they finally melt.

Shown here is the Canada Glacier.

Ice shelves

Along some parts of the Antarctic coastline, the ice cap reaches out over the water. It forms a large, floating sheet of ice called an ice shelf. Ice shelves can cover great stretches of water. The Ross Ice Shelf covers an area almost as large as Arizona and Colorado together. On the outer edge of an ice shelf, great cliffs of ice tower over the sea, making it difficult for ships to stop there. The outer parts of an ice shelf often break away to form wide, flat icebergs.

Mountains and valleys

Not all of Antarctica is covered with ice. Some mountain peaks stick out above the ice cap. Antarctica's longest chain of mountains are the Transantarctic Mountains, which cross the entire continent. Transantarctic peaks can reach more than 14,100 feet (4,300 meters) high. The region of the Transantarctic Mountains includes some large areas that are not covered by ice. These areas are called dry valleys. Dry valleys are mainly covered with bare rock instead of ice. However, there are some lakes in dry valleys, and these are permanently covered by ice more than ten feet (three meters) deep.

Diary of a continent

▶ **200 million years ago**
Antarctica is part of the Gondwana supercontinent, along with Australia, Africa, and South America.

▶ **150 million years ago**
Gondwana breaks up.

▶ **40 million years ago**
Antarctica breaks away from Australia and drifts closer to the South Pole.

▶ **10 million years ago**
Antarctica grows very cold, with huge glaciers forming.

▶ **5 million years ago**
Most of the continent is covered with ice. Its land animals die out.

▶ **1820**
Antarctica is first sighted by ship.

▶ **1911**
Roald Amundsen becomes the first person to reach the South Pole.

Mt. Erebus—on Ross Island in Antarctica—is the world's southernmost active volcano.

Climate, Plants, and Animals

Climate

Temperatures are always cold in Antarctica. The coldest region of the continent is inland, where winter temperatures have been recorded below –112 °F (–80 °C). The inland is also the driest region of Antarctica, with no rain and little snowfall. Coastal areas are milder, with some rain and summers that are warm enough to melt and clear the ice in certain areas. However, even on the coast, the temperatures are still cold. Only on some of the islands do summer temperatures rise above 32 °F (0 °C). Antarctica is not only cold, but very windy. Blizzards are common and wind speeds can exceed 186 miles (300 kilometers) per hour. The wind makes the temperatures seem even colder.

Lichen can grow on bare rocks, as shown here.

Hardy plants

Only small, hardy plants, such as grass or moss, can survive in Antarctica. They grow mainly along the ice-free parts of the coast. There are also **lichen** and algae, which can survive in much colder regions. Lichen can grow in the cracks of inland rocks and algae can grow in snow and ice.

Swimmers and fliers

Like most Antarctic plants, animals of this continent live near the coast or on islands. The only animals that live permanently on land are small **invertebrates** such as **midges** and flies. Most of the larger animals swim or fly, and get their main food supply from the sea. Some of them **migrate** to warmer areas during the winter. These animals include seals, penguins, gulls, and terns. Most of them eat fish, although some of them prey on other birds or seals. All these animals have layers of fat, fur, or feathers on their bodies to keep them warm. **Parasites** such as lice, mites, and ticks often keep warm by living on birds or seals.

Antarctic seals have thick layers of fat to keep them warm.

Marine animals

Life is abundant in Antarctic seas. The most common animal near Antarctica is **krill,** a tiny shrimplike creature that moves through the water in huge swarms. Krill is important, because many other marine animals feed on it, and because large amounts of krill are caught and sold as food for people. Other Antarctic marine animals include squid, fish, and a variety of whales.

Land and sea
- leopard seal
- southern elephant seal
- Weddell seal
- Ross seal
- crabeater seal
- Antarctic fur seal
- Adélie penguin
- emperor penguin
- chinstrap penguin
- gentoo penguin
- king penguin
- macaroni penguin

Air, land and sea
- wandering albatross
- Antarctic petrel
- giant petrel
- snow petrel
- storm petrel
- Cape pigeon
- southern fulmar
- brown skua
- sheathbill
- Dominican gull
- Antarctic tern

Antarctic ocean
- sperm whale
- killer whale
- southern bottlenose whale
- southern fourtooth whale
- blue whale
- fin whale
- humpback whale
- minke whale
- right whale
- sei whale
- icefish
- plunderfish
- Antarctic cod
- squid
- krill

Wandering albatross live on Albatross Island, South Georgia.

19

Discovery and Exploration

People knew about Antarctica long before it was discovered. Ancient Greek thinkers reasoned that there was a great **landmass** on the southern extreme of Earth, but they could not agree what it was like. No one could prove Antarctica existed until 1820, when ships finally drew near enough to sight it. The first people to set foot on the continent were probably seal or whale hunters. They were followed by explorers from many countries, including England, Australia, and the United States. Early explorations of Antarctica occurred along its coastline. Serious exploration of the inland region began in 1901, when a great race began to see who could reach the South Pole first.

Reaching the South Pole

Conditions were harsh and dangerous for early Antarctic explorers. With no modern transportation and little protection from the cold, they had to face the dangers of **frostbite,** blizzards, and rough **terrain.** In December 1911, two exploring parties began to close in on the South Pole. One was a British party led by Robert F. Scott. The other was a Norwegian party led by Roald Amundsen. Amundsen's party was traveling more efficiently and won the race on December 14, 1911. Scott's party did not reach the South Pole until January 25, 1912. Although Amundsen returned safely to the coast, Scott's entire party died on their return trip, trapped by a blizzard between food supply stations. A research station at the South Pole has been named after the two parties' leaders—the Amundsen-Scott base.

Research stations

Antarctica still has no true towns or cities, but it does have more than 30 research stations, including one over the South Pole. These research stations house scientists, pilots, and technicians—sometimes hundreds of them. No one lives at the stations permanently. They are maintained by countries including Great Britain, Australia, New Zealand, Argentina, Russia, and the United States.

Some of these countries have claimed large regions of Antarctica as their territory. Even so, relations between people from different countries on Antarctica are open and friendly, without strict border patrols. The countries have agreed to keep military conflict and nuclear weapons out of Antarctica, not to allow mining, and to protect **native** plants and animals.

Facts about living in
Antarctica

- Many places in Antarctica are named after its early explorers, such as the Ross Ice Shelf, the Ellsworth Mountains, and the Amundsen-Scott base at the South Pole.

- Antarctic research stations are maintained throughout the year. They are busiest during the summer. The largest is McMurdo Station, which can have a summer population of 1,000.

- No mining takes place in Antarctica, although petroleum, coal, and other valuable minerals can be found there.

- A limited amount of fishing is allowed in Antarctic seas.

British researchers collect data near Australia's Davis research station.

This map shows where the permanent Antarctic research stations are located.

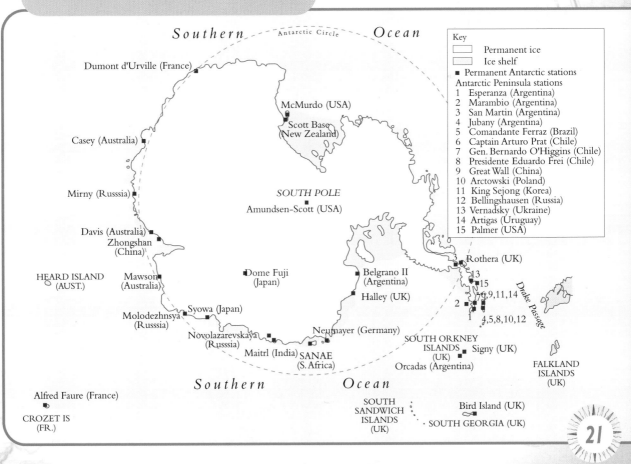

Key

☐ Permanent ice
☐ Ice shelf
■ Permanent Antarctic stations

Antarctic Peninsula stations
1 Esperanza (Argentina)
2 Marambio (Argentina)
3 San Martin (Argentina)
4 Jubany (Argentina)
5 Comandante Ferraz (Brazil)
6 Captain Arturo Prat (Chile)
7 Gen. Bernardo O'Higgins (Chile)
8 Presidente Eduardo Frei (Chile)
9 Great Wall (China)
10 Arctowski (Poland)
11 King Sejong (Korea)
12 Bellingshausen (Russia)
13 Vernadsky (Ukraine)
14 Artigas (Uruguay)
15 Palmer (USA)

Southern   Antarctic Circle   *Ocean*

Dumont d'Urville (France)

McMurdo (USA)
Scott Base (New Zealand)

Casey (Australia)

Mirny (Russsia)

SOUTH POLE
Amundsen-Scott (USA)

Davis (Australia)
Zhongshan (China)

HEARD ISLAND (AUST.)

Mawson (Australia)

Dome Fuji (Japan)

Belgrano II (Argentina)
Halley (UK)

Rothera (UK)
13
15
7,6,9,11,14
2
1   4,5,8,10,12

Drake Passage

Molodezhnsya (Russsia)
Syowa (Japan)

Novolazarevskaya (Russsia)
Maitrl (India)
SANAE (S. Africa)

Neumayer (Germany)

SOUTH ORKNEY ISLANDS (UK)   Signy (UK)
Orcadas (Argentina)

FALKLAND ISLANDS (UK)

Alfred Faure (France)

CROZET IS (FR.)

Southern   *Ocean*

SOUTH SANDWICH ISLANDS (UK)

Bird Island (UK)
SOUTH GEORGIA (UK)

The Making of ISLAND CONTINENTS

Australia and Antarctica are island continents. Because they are island continents, they are **isolated** from other continents. This makes it difficult for plants, animals, and people from other continents to cross over to the island continents. Australia and Antarctica are the only island continents today, but this was not always so. Every continent has been an island continent during some period in prehistoric times. For example, around 30 million years ago, South America was an island continent.

Before Australia and Antarctica became island continents, they were joined to the ancient supercontinent of Gondwana. Africa and South America were also joined with Gondwana, and all four continents shared the same kinds of wildlife. What caused these continents to join together? What caused them to break apart? These questions puzzled scientists for many years. They finally have found some answers.

Moving tectonic plates split Australia and Antarctica apart about 40 million years ago.

Giant plates

Before the mid-1900s, most people had a false idea about the continents. They believed that the continents stood motionless on Earth, in the same place for billions of years. About 50 years ago, scientists discovered that the continents were actually moving. In fact, they have moved constantly since ancient times, and are still moving today.

Around the 1960s, scientists discovered that the continents are attached to huge plates of rock, called **tectonic** plates. Together, the different plates make up the entire solid surface of Earth. They fit together like a giant jigsaw puzzle. Many plates are larger than the continents, because they contain huge sections of Earth's **crust** that include the ocean floor. Despite their large size, tectonic plates move very slowly over Earth and can cover great distances over millions of years. The way the continents move is called plate tectonics. The study of plate tectonics helps us understand the changing position of continents and how island continents form.

Plates in motion

Tectonic plates are made up of rock from Earth's crust and upper **mantle**. Each plate is about 60 miles (100 kilometers) thick. The plates float on a layer of rocks, moving sideways along a hot lower surface. When the plates move, anything attached to them moves as well, including continents and parts of the ocean floor. This movement is very slow—about 4 inches (10 centimeters) every year—but the plates can cover great distances over millions of years.

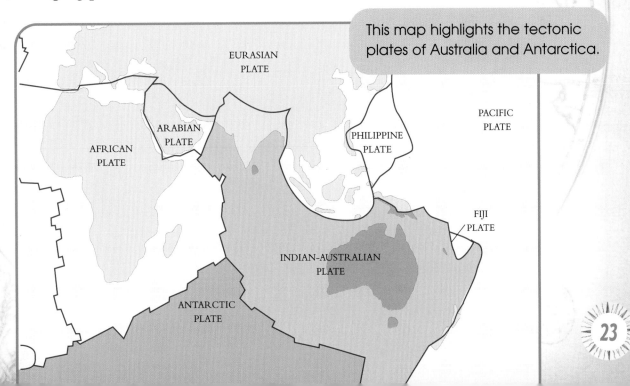

This map highlights the tectonic plates of Australia and Antarctica.

EURASIAN PLATE

ARABIAN PLATE

AFRICAN PLATE

PHILIPPINE PLATE

PACIFIC PLATE

FIJI PLATE

INDIAN-AUSTRALIAN PLATE

ANTARCTIC PLATE

Plate **tectonics** help us understand how continents slowly move across Earth's surface. When the plates carry two continents toward each other, they may eventually connect with each other. When the plates carry the continents apart, island continents are more likely to form.

Pangaea

Australia and Antarctica were not island continents about 250 million years ago. In fact, at that time there were no island continents anywhere on Earth. All of the continents were pushed together into a giant supercontinent called Pangaea.

The name *Pangaea* comes from a Greek phrase meaning "all land." Gondwana existed during this period of time, but not as a separate supercontinent. It formed the southern part of Pangaea. Gondwana was made up of five great **landmasses**—Australia, Antarctica, Africa, South America, and India. Europe, Asia, and North America were joined together to make up the northern section of Pangaea, called Laurasia.

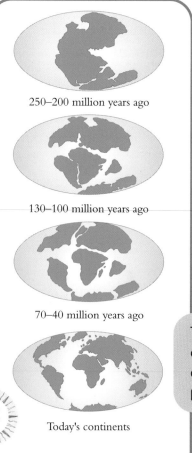

250–200 million years ago

130–100 million years ago

70–40 million years ago

Today's continents

Regional differences

The regions of Gondwana and Laurasia were different from each other in many ways. Gondwana had many prehistoric plants and animals that were not found in most of Laurasia. These included animals such as Lystrosaurus, a hippopotamus-like reptile, and plants such as Glossopteris, a plant with tongue-shaped leaves. Even the **climate** of these two regions was different. For millions of years, much of Laurasia lay in Earth's warm, **tropical** zone. At the same time, much of Gondwana lay closer to the freezing South Pole, which was covered by huge **glaciers.**

The giant supercontinent called Pangaea broke apart slowly, over a long period of time.

Break-up and isolation

By 200 million years ago, the plates below Pangaea began to break it apart. Laurasia and Gondwana became two smaller supercontinents. Australia was in a remote part of Gondwana and was getting more **isolated** at this time. Antarctica still had a more central position closer to the other Gondwana continents. By 150 million years ago, Gondwana and Laurasia were breaking up into the continents we know today. However, Australia and Antarctica remained connected for a long time. They finally separated and became island continents about 40 million years ago.

When continents break apart from each other, they may become island continents. But they do not always stay that way. When Africa and South America broke away from the other Gondwana continents, they drifted toward the northern continents. Millions of years later, South America joined to North America, and Africa joined to Asia. India was another Gondwana landmass that drifted north, eventually joining with Asia. Although India is not recognized as a separate continent, it is often called a **subcontinent.**

This is a **fossil** of Glossopteris, an ancient plant with tongue-shaped leaves, that was common on the Gondwana supercontinent.

Lystrosaurus was a hippo-shaped reptile of ancient Gondwana.

Changes in
CLIMATE

The movement of **tectonic** plates has changed Australia and Antarctica many times over the past 300 million years. These two continents have been joined to each other, then pushed into a supercontinent, then split into island continents.

As a continent changes position, other changes occur, such as changes in **climate.** For example, if a continent in the **temperate** zone drifts into a **tropical** zone, the climate will grow much warmer. However, not all changes in climate are caused by a continent's movement. Some climate changes are global, and affect large parts of Earth. This happened during the last **Ice Age,** when world temperatures became much colder.

Different directions

Gondwana had completely broken up about 60 million years ago. However, Australia and Antarctica were still joined together deep in the **Southern Hemisphere.** Both continents shared the same kinds of birds, reptiles, **amphibians,** small mammals, and freshwater fish. Both continents had the same wet climate, with large areas of shady rain forest. By 30 million years ago, Australia and Antarctica had completely split apart. Although they still shared many of the same kinds of plants and animals, these two island continents were moving in different directions. Australia began drifting north. Antarctica drifted deeper into the Southern Hemisphere.

Temperate rain forests once covered much of Australia and Antarctica, but only rarely occur in Australia today.

By five million years ago, Australia's climate became mainly warm and dry. Most of the rain forest plants and animals had disappeared. They were replaced by woodland, grassland, and desert wildlife. During the ice age that began about two million years ago, Australia's climate became colder for a while. **Glaciers** developed in the southern part of the continent. But when that ice age ended, the glaciers vanished, and most of the continent became warm and dry again.

Something very different happened to Antarctica. Antarctica drifted farther into the South Pole region. Glaciers began to grow on Antarctica after it broke away from Australia and, by 10 million years ago, they formed a thick ice cap over much of the continent. By five million years ago, it was too cold for most plants and animals to survive on land, and nearly all of the continent became buried by ice.

Future climates

Australia and Antarctica are still being moved by tectonic plates. Both continents are likely to drift north. About 50 million years from now, Australia will be much closer to the **equator,** and may even connect with Asia. Heavy rain will fall over a wider area of the Australian continent. Huge desert regions will turn into rain forests again. The Antarctic climate will go through even more drastic changes as it drifts north. About 180 million years from now, the Antarctic ice cap will melt, rivers will flow, and the land will again be occupied by a wide variety of plants and animals.

Australia's climate became mainly warm and dry about five million years ago.

Isolation and
WILDLIFE

When Australia and Antarctica were part of Pangaea, they shared the same kinds of wildlife with all other continents. However, after becoming island continents, they developed different kinds of plants and animals. This happened during the **Age of Mammals,** a time when large and small mammals became common throughout the world. Many different kinds of mammals became widespread at this time, including prehistoric cats, bears, elephants, horses, camels, and deer. But none of these large land mammals inhabited Australia or Antarctica. They had no way of reaching these **isolated** continents.

Ancient marsupials

Ancient Australia was inhabited by a wide variety of **marsupials,** or pouched mammals. They included giant kangaroos and wombats and a huge creature called Diprotodon. Although these giants are now extinct, many more familiar marsupials still survive. There are also some mammals without pouches—including seals, bats, mice, and dingoes—that managed to enter Australia.

Ancient Diprotodon was the largest marsupial ever to live.

Cold-weather animals

Prehistoric animals that lived in Antarctica were also isolated from other continents. But even if animals from other continents could have reached Antarctica, most would have died from the cold. Only animals such as seals, penguins, and small insects could survive the freezing weather.

End of isolation

Australia and Antarctica may still be island continents, but since the arrival of Europeans, they are no longer as isolated as they once were. European animals have been brought to these continents, sometimes causing great harm to the **native** wildlife. People have hunted the lands of Australia and fished the seas of both continents.

Protecting wildlife

Today, there is more pressure to preserve the wildlife of the island continents. Many Australian native plants and animals are now protected by law, and there are more national parks and nature reserves where wildlife cannot be hunted. There are also strict laws controlling the kinds of plants and animals that can be brought into the country.

Australia's first European settlers did not appreciate the continent's unique plants and animals. They cut down many of the native eucalyptus and acacia trees and replaced them with European trees such as oak, willow, and poplar. They killed many of the marsupials and caused some to become extinct. They allowed European animals to overrun the land. These settlers actually wanted to destroy the native plants and animals and turn Australia into a country like England or Scotland. Today, however, people living in Australia take more care with their continent's unique wildlife.

Environmental groups from all over the world are concerned about the future of Antarctica. They put pressure on governments to ban whale hunting and to prevent overfishing in the seas. They also want a guarantee that the continent will never be used for mining or military activity.

Events like this tree planting show how Australians take pride in their plants and animals.

GLOSSARY

Age of Mammals time in Earth's history from about 65 million years ago to the present when mammals became the most common animals

Age of Reptiles time in Earth's history about 250 to 65 million years ago when reptiles such as dinosaurs were the largest living animals

alpine high mountain region

amphibian four-legged animal that lays its eggs in water

bauxite mineral mined for the aluminum it contains

climate kind of weather that occurs in a particular region

convict someone who has been found guilty of a crime

crust Earth's outermost rock layer, about 5 to 45 miles (8 to 70 kilometers) thick

drought period of time when water is scarce

elevation height above sea level

equator imaginary line around the middle of Earth's surface

erosion way landforms are worn away by water, wind, or ice

evergreen tree with leaves or needles that stay green all the time, such as that of pines, acacias, or eucalyptus trees

famine severe shortage of food in a place

fertile rich in nutrients

frostbite injury caused by exposure of the skin to extreme cold

geographer person who studies Earth's surface

glacier mass of ice that moves slowly across the land

ice age time when parts of Earth become colder and are covered by glaciers. There have been many ice ages, but the most recent Ice Age ended over 10,000 years ago.

iceberg mass of floating ice

invertebrate animal that does not have a backbone

iron ore mineral mined for the iron it contains

isolated set apart from others

krill small, shrimp-like animals of the ocean

land bridge area of land that connects two continents

landmass large area of land, such as a continent

lichen plant-like form of life that can grow on rock or wood, and needs little moisture to survive

livestock farm animals, such as cattle, pigs and chickens

mantle layer of rock about 1,800 miles (2,900 kilometers) thick that lies below Earth's crust

marsupial mammal that carries its young in a pouch

midge very small, flying insect

migrate move from one area to another

monotreme mammal that lays eggs

native originally from an area

nomadic traveling or roaming

Northern Hemisphere northern half of Earth between the North Pole and the equator

parasite living thing that lives on or in a plant or animal and takes nourishment from it

pharmaceuticals drugs or medicines

Southern Hemisphere southern half of Earth between the South Pole and the equator

standard of living level of goods and income enjoyed by a society

subcontinent large landmass that forms a section of a continent

tectonic relating to the structure and changes in Earth's crust

temperate moderate; not permanently hot or cold

terrain section of land, especially with reference to its natural features

timber wood that is useful for construction

tropical of the tropics, the warm regions around the equator

FURTHER READING

Petersen, David. *Africa.* Danbury, Conn.: Children's Press, 1998.

Petersen, David. *Antarctica.* Danbury, Conn.: Children's Press, 1998.

Petersen, David. *Asia.* Danbury, Conn.: Children's Press, 1998.

Petersen, David. *Australia.* Danbury, Conn.: Children's Press, 1998.

Petersen, David. *Europe.* Danbury, Conn.: Children's Press, 1998.

Petersen, David. *North America.* Danbury, Conn.: Children's Press, 1998.

Petersen, David. *South America.* Danbury, Conn.: Children's Press, 1998.

INDEX